Original title:
The Last Leaf on the Shelf

Copyright © 2025 Creative Arts Management OÜ
All rights reserved.

Author: Maya Livingston
ISBN HARDBACK: 978-1-80581-829-8
ISBN PAPERBACK: 978-1-80581-356-9
ISBN EBOOK: 978-1-80581-829-8

Remains of the Forgotten

On the shelf so high and tight,
A leaf that's lost its vibrant light.
It curls and bends, a funny sight,
A relic of past autumn's flight.

With dust bunnies as its close friends,
It giggles while the daylight ends.
In a world where no one tends,
A comedic tale, the humor blends.

Once it danced in zephyrs bold,
Now it's stuck, so brittle and old.
A green dream turned to a joke retold,
A punchline wrapped in memories cold.

And thus it sits, quite unaware,
While shelf mates pretend not to care.
Its laughter echoes through the air,
A leaf lost, yet beyond compare.

The Final Farewell of a Breath

A gasp escapes from dusty tome,
A forgotten breath, it calls home.
With each tick, it starts to roam,
A farewell dance in quiet chrome.

It puffed and wheezed, a jolly prank,
In the corners of a spindly flank.
As whispers rise, the laughter drank,
A comedy show that no one sank.

Through pages tattered, stories flow,
A vent of laughs from long ago.
With every sigh, a spark to glow,
The final breath steals all the show.

Leaves tumble down in comical spree,
As if they know the end is free.
Yet, in this room, so wild and glee,
A breath bids adieu with a chuckle, whee!

Emblems of Time's Gentle Passage

In the attic, things lie still,
Cobwebs dance with a ghostly thrill.
Dust bunnies roll with laughter loud,
As time winks beneath a shroud.

Old chairs creak, they tell their tales,
Of picnics and runaway snails.
Each corner holds its silly score,
As whispers flutter, wanting more.

The Circa of Almost Forgotten Joys

Once a hat, now just a hat rack,
It dreams of days when it had flair and knack.
Forgotten socks in pairs, quite wild,
Grin as they bask in memories piled.

The clock ticks on with goofy chimes,
Counting giggles, mishaps, and rhymes.
Each tick a nudge, a friendly tease,
As laughter echoes through the trees.

Tones of Twilight's Embrace

Silly shadows dance on walls,
Playing tag, forgetting calls.
A teacup spins, a saucer flies,
In twilight's glow, a ruckus lies.

The breeze carries whispers, quite absurd,
Of dancing ants and chicken heard.
As colors swirl in a playful caper,
Giggles rise like fragrant paper.

The Sigh Before the Stillness

Creaking doors unlock a grin,
As socks embark on a spinning spin.
The chairs all chuckle as they plot,
To catch a glimpse of the silly lot.

Beneath the shelf, things long forgot,
A puzzle piece, a treasured spot.
With every sigh, a new tale starts,
Each flutter of dust steals our hearts.

A Tattered Tale Unspooled

Once bright and bold, now aged and frayed,
A story hangs, in sunlight laid.
Who left it there, all warped and bent?
A mystery curled, not heaven-sent.

Dust bunnies dance, with whimsical grace,
As I tiptoe past this curious place.
The words may fade, the ink may smear,
But laughter remains, oh my dear!

The Weight of Unraveled Dreams

A dream once stitched with threads of gold,
Now tangled thoughts, or so I'm told.
With each pull, it goes awry,
'Tis a cloak of whimsy, oh my!

The stitches laugh, as they come undone,
In the fabric of life, we find our fun.
A patchwork quilt, with bits of jest,
In this cluttered world, I find my rest.

Nature's Final Gesture

A lone twig sways, in the breeze, quite bold,
It waves goodbye, as autumn's gold.
With a wink and a nudge, it leaves the team,
And falls to the ground, as if in a dream.

The critters all giggle, the branches play pranks,
As the wind howls softly, and nature laughs thanks.
What's left behind? Oh just a leaf,
A reminder it's fun, not dwell on grief.

A Capsule of Old Stories

In a corner sits, a jar of delight,
Filled with tales from the cozy night.
Each whimsy word, a smirk in disguise,
Unfolding truths with giggling sighs.

Pick one at random, let laughter ignite,
As adventures unfold, under pale moonlight.
These stories old bend and twist,
In a playful dance, they can't be missed.

The Browning Ribbons of Time

In a book so old, pages worn,
Dust bunnies dance, they're never torn.
Ribbons fade, oh what a sight,
As bookshelves giggle, both day and night.

A cat sleeps on the corner edge,
Dreaming of mice and a cozy hedge.
With a yawn that shakes the very spine,
He swears these stories could be divine.

Monocles slide down a nose of great age,
As stories tumble off the page.
An author's pen still holds a grudge,
With plots so thick, they start to smudge.

Yet here we are, with memories tight,
The smell of old paper a pure delight.
So let us laugh with pages anew,
While ribbons unravel, and time takes its cue.

Wistful Thoughts of What Remains

A teacup cracked, still holds some tea,
A memory winks, oh wouldn't it be?
To sip on wisdom, just once more,
But all we find is crumbs galore.

Jars of sweets with lids so tight,
We peek inside, oh what a sight!
A moth flutters, in search of a snack,
While candy wrappers begin to crack.

Time marches on, it has no shame,
But here we giggle, oh what a game!
With remnants of laughter echoing clear,
Each dusty corner brings us near.

So toast to the ruins of yesterday's grace,
As we find the humor in this slow race.
With wistful thoughts, we gently remain,
In the cadence of laughter, skipping the pain.

The Heartbeat of Diminishing Days

Tick-tock goes the clock on the wall,
Whispers of moments, both big and small.
A half-eaten pie left on the plate,
Invites a debate, was it fate?

Webs in the corners, dust in the air,
Pondering who really does care?
A tickle from time, oh what a tease,
As we shuffle thoughts, with such great ease.

The calendar's quirks, oh isn't it fun?
Days slip away, like they're on the run.
With silly reminders and dying light,
We laugh at our clocks, just out of spite.

So cherish the days, as they flicker and sway,
With laughter as our guide, come what may.
Each heartbeat counts down with an awkward sway,
Diminishing days, in the funniest way.

The Solitary Reminder of Bright

A lone paperclip, shiny and bright,
Stands guard on the desk, a curious sight.
Holding papers, dreams, and a half-written plan,
Who knew it'd help us, the oddball fan?

The comfort of chaos, oh how we thrive,
With mismatched socks, we feel so alive.
A laugh, a snicker, is always the best,
As we organize chaos, we cannot rest.

A glass of water, half full today,
Catches the sunlight in a playful way.
We toast to the spills, the crumbs, the dust,
In the solitary glow, it's all a must.

So here's to reminders, both silly and grand,
That life's little quirks are just what we planned.
With laughter our beacon, we're never alone,
In this vibrant mess, we've lovingly grown.

The Last Glisten of Green

One tiny sprout hangs by a thread,
It squints at sunshine, bright but dead.
Each morning I check its sturdy stance,
Hoping it sways, doing a dance.

In the next room, a cactus grins,
Boasting that it never gives in.
While I'm here, my plant takes a chance,
Fading away, not quite in a trance.

A water drop dangles, oh so sly,
Like it's flirting with the great, big sky.
As my hopes rise for a leafy spree,
The dust bunnies laugh, 'Let it be free!'

But I still cheer for that little green chap,
With a throne of dust, it's a brave map.
So I water, I wait, and I scheme,
For the next little green will fulfill my dream!

Fragile Hopes in a Dusty Corner

In a corner, forgotten and grim,
Lies a pot where the hopes once did brim.
A whisper of green fights for its fate,
In a dance-off with dust—it's first rate!

Scraggly leaves, sticking out like a tease,
Waving gently in the warm, dusty breeze.
Tired of waiting, I give it a name—
'Hopeful Harold'—this plant is to blame!

Each day I joke, 'It's the last of its kind!'
While contemplating how to unwind.
Yet Harold the brave, he's taken the lead,
With aspirations, he knows how to plead.

I pat his head as I turn to depart,
He tickles my nose, this ridiculous art.
In that dusty corner, his sparkle does shine,
Fragile but fierce, my green buddy divine!

Dancing with the Dust

A waltz with dust bunnies, my plant takes the floor,
While I sit nearby, laughing more and more.
With a twirl and a spin, it leans to the left,
Declaring its moves, like a dancer's cleft.

I broke out the snacks, some crumbs on the shelf,
'Come join the party!' I hollered, 'Be yourself!'
But the dust starts to gather, oh what a scene,
My plant's strutting around, it's making a scene!

It sways to the rhythm of a windy old tune,
While I clap along, sharing crumbs with a broom.
"Dust off your shoulders!" I shout with a grin,
"My dear little friend, let the party begin!"

But as the night wanes, and the laughter fades,
The leaf waves goodbye, while the dust parade wades.
Though it may not be grand in the grandest sense,
Together we laughed, which felt so immense!

Color of Farewell

A hint of green bids a quirky adieu,
As I watch the last blush, a fitting view.
'Twas a saga of growth, now a tale to tell,
In the colorful hues, I wish him farewell.

With a wink to the sunlight, he flickers his grin,
Then wobbles a bit, as if to begin.
I chuckle to think how he lived in the dream,
Now off to explore the great plant-themed scheme.

Each crinkle of leaf, an echo from past,
Recalls all the moments too wild to last.
'Twas a short little journey, but oh so sweet,
In the heart of this room, he danced on his feet.

As I hug the pot, my dear leafy mate,
It's goodbye for now, with a twist of fate.
I'll keep his memory nestled so well,
In the laughter and color of our farewell!

Fading Echoes of Autumn's End

The branches dance, a lively jig,
A leaf hangs on, looking big.
It's clinging tight, what a sight!
Old friends chuckle, 'Hold on tight!'

The winds tease it with a playful shove,
'Are you still here?' it says, 'I love!'
With every gust, a wobbly twirl,
The leaf gives in, what a whirl!

The squirrels gather, what a ruckus,
'Let's play catch!' the leaf disputes.
Yet every throw just goes amiss,
Each aims for glory, no hit or bliss!

At last, it drops, a graceful flop,
Laughing still as its friends stop.
In so many ways, it sparked delight,
'Next year, pals, I'll be back for a flight!'

Whispers of Forgotten Seasons

A bottle cap sits on the sill,
An old shoe too, a kooky thrill.
'What a crew!' the dust bunnies hoot,
'Let's play charades, who's the root?'

The shadows stretch in the evening glow,
As autumn leaves begin their show.
One tipsy drop leaves cackling hue,
'It's just a leaf, what's it to you?'

A paper plane flies high, then dips,
'Take a lesson from those leaf tips!'
Yet laughter fades, it drifts away,
Toward a new home, come what may!

In the old house, where echoes dwell,
A new leaf forms on a wishing well.
'Next round's on me!' it giggles bright,
As whispers flutter into the night.

Fragile Remnants of Time

Once a leaf, played every part,
Now it changes, just like art.
'Take a snap!' a few kids shout,
Before it fades, without a doubt.

His buddies shout, 'You'll not be missed!'
'Oh come on, guys,' it starts to hiss.
Well worn stories from yesteryear,
The leaf just chuckles, holding dear.

Wind invites it for a spin,
'Join the fun! No way to win!'
With every loop, it laughs aglow,
'This round's for me, let's go, let's go!'

But time runs on, and it must fall,
Leaving behind a light-hearted call.
'Farewell, dear friends, I'll take a bow!'
In every giggle, it's living now!

The Faintest Brush of Change

A spot of yellow, bright and bold,
Grabs the sun, as autumn's told.
Friends around it make a fuss,
'How can you laugh, oh little plus?'

Tickle the breeze, it swirls just right,
The little leaf launches from its height.
It twirls and spins, in a brazen mood,
Painting the air, in playful brood.

But squirrels peek through their tiny doors,
'That leaf's got moves, give it applause!'
With nuts all stacked, they shriek and cheer,
Departure of autumn draws closer near.

A giggling huddle, a make-believe,
'Tis but a game, let's not grieve.'
And as it drops, a final refrain,
The dance is over, till springtime's gain!

Farewell in the Symphony of Decay

In the twilight of autumn's show,
Lies a tale of what we used to know.
Branches quiver, a breeze hums low,
One leaf clings on, stealing the show.

The squirrels gather, planning their feast,
Chattering loudly, they won't be ceased.
But one brave leaf, feeling the least,
Holds on tight, to become a beast.

A gust comes by, oh what a jest,
It twirls around, giving a test.
The leaf hangs on, it knows it's blessed,
In this comedy, quite unimpressed.

And as the sun dips into the night,
The laughter echoes, what a sight!
The leaf that remains, a quirky delight,
In this symphony, it's taking flight.

The Blend of Past and Present

Once a flurry of colors so bright,
Now it's just brown, losing its fight.
But there it clings with all its might,
A relic of chaos, in autumn's light.

Memories whisper from far-off trees,
Of summer's laughter carried by the breeze.
Yet here it wobbles, like a clown with fleas,
Daring the world to catch it with ease.

Old tales told in the rustle and caw,
Branch in hand, it breaks the last law.
With every giggle, the bark will draw,
A marathon of gags, what a raw flaw!

As winter approaches with icy hands,
The leaf has plans, it makes its stands.
And in its final dance, fate expands,
A mix of giggles, and cold reprimands.

The Hanging Shade of Yesterday

Once majestic, now haggard and pale,
Still hanging on, like a tired old tale.
Winds tease gently, giving a wail,
But it's here for the laughs, not to bail.

It sways and swings in a funny old groove,
Daring the weather to make it move.
A shadow of what might have been, a prove,
That even in decline, we can still improve.

The daylight mocks with a glittering grin,
As if to say, "Where have you been?"
But it chuckles back with quirky spin,
"I'm here to party, let's begin!"

So here it hangs, a memory's shade,
With hopes of laughter, the jester is made.
In the game of life, it's unafraid,
For in the end, we all get played.

A Reflection on Nature's Canvas

Upon the branch, a canvas remains,
Painted with laughter, and whimsical stains.
One lone leaf, defies the mundane,
Flaunts its wrinkles, like old refrains.

The days grow shorter, shadows extend,
With a personality that just won't bend.
It flaps like a flag, making a friend,
In the theater of life, it takes the blend.

Fickle winds blow, the backdrop of fate,
Yet it giggles back, it won't hesitate.
In the sitcom of seasons, it plays its state,
Making the chilly air, its ultimate mate.

So let the sun set, let the moon rise,
Our hero up there, to everyone's surprise,
In the laughter of leaves sits the greatest prize,
That even decay can be quite the guise.

The Unraveling Thread in the Fabric of Time

A sock disagrees with the other pair,
It says, "Why not dance? I swear!"
With yarn in knots and a playful twist,
They chart a course, no turn to miss.

The shirt, it chuckles from the back,
"You think you're funny? What a quack!"
But wear and tear set to a tune,
As buttons pop, a wild festoon.

The jeans, they laugh; their fabric worn,
"We're fashion statements since the morn!"
But every stitch holds tales of yore,
In laughter sweet, they yearn for more.

So time just spins in fabric's play,
As threads of joy begin to fray.
With each loose end, a tale unfolds,
Life's pattern bright, in stitches bold.

Afterglow of What Once Was

The sun-photographed a winter's leaf,
It giggles now, despite the grief.
Once green and bold, now crispy brown,
It dreams of summers, not of frown.

A once proud flower whispers low,
"I bloomed so bright, where did I go?"
The bees still buzz, all in good cheer,
Reminding her, she's still held dear.

Old potpourri dreams of the past,
Scented whispers, though fading fast.
Cousin dust joins the merry crew,
And sends a wink, "I miss you too!"

They dance on shelves, both near and far,
Recalling days when they were a star.
In afterglow, the laughter flows,
For memories shine, where friendship grows.

A Sigh Among the Shadows

In corners dark where shadows loom,
A sigh escaped, through dust, it bloomed.
A light bulb flickered on and off,
"Stop that now, you pesky scoff!"

The clock chimed in, its gears all squeaked,
"Old friend, your silence seems quite weak!"
The broom just giggled, sweeping grime,
"That sigh's just hope, caught out of time."

With vacuum's roar, there came a fuss,
A battle fought, to ride the bus.
"They should all join!" the shadows cried,
"Together we can turn the tide!"

So here they laugh, despite the gloom,
Their banter dances in the room.
A sigh, a laugh, the shadows play,
Each cast in light finds joy today.

The Final Sketch of Nature's Palette

A brush dipped deep in colors bright,
Nature says with a cheeky bite.
"Let's add some pink to the old gray tree,
A splash of joy for all to see!"

Clouds in whispers, cotton candy,
"Who ordered that? Oh, isn't it dandy?"
As rain bows down, it giggles wide,
While puddles dance, they just can't hide.

The sun grins big, a golden show,
Painting laughter for the world to know.
"Bring in the blue," the river calls,
"Let's sprinkle joy, let's have a ball!"

So nature's canvas, wild and free,
Is filled with glee; come paint with me!
In every stroke, a jest, a cheer,
Life's final art, forever near.

The Last Gasp of Vibrant Days

Old Barry's got a tattered hat,
It sparkles like a tired cat.
Each joke he tells is worn and frayed,
But laughter follows, unafraid.

His friends, they squint at sunset light,
Dreaming of days when they felt bright.
Yet every time they try to boast,
They end up laughing, that's the most.

The chair they saved for twenty years,
Now creaks and groans with laughter's cheers.
They dance around with giddy glee,
As if the world's a comedy.

So raise your glass and toast the show,
To vibrant days we kind of know.
With silly hats and giggles loud,
We celebrate, a quirky crowd.

Serenade of the Almost Gone

In the corner sits a remnant small,
With stories wrapped in silent thrall.
Its colors fade, a bit like me,
But still it hums a memory.

Once it danced in vibrant hues,
Now it wears a coat of blues.
Yet if you listen close at night,
It sings of joy, it sings of light.

Old drafts of laughter linger near,
As if to conjure what was dear.
The barely-there will always tease,
And leave us guessing with a sneeze.

So strum your heart and let it strut,
Celebrate the weird and the rut.
For in the end, it's quite a show,
This serenade of almost so.

Breadcrumbs of Youth's Memory

A breadcrumb trail of days gone by,
Each step a giggle, a little sigh.
The mischief found in pocketed stones,
Now leads to tales of wild unknowns.

In every crumb a secret hid,
From treehouse dreams to laughing kids.
We chase the echoes down the lane,
And gather quirks like grains of grain.

A half-eaten pie shall tell the tale,
Of how we raced the summer gale.
With each new bite, a memory blooms,
Like springtime flowers in busy rooms.

So save the crumbs and share the laughs,
For youth sprinkles joy on mismatched paths.
As we look back through time's embrace,
These breadcrumbs lead us to our place.

Shadows of What Was Once Bright

In the glow of aging lights,
Shadows dance on fuzzy nights.
Once electric, now just a spark,
Turning whispers into a lark.

Faded glories on the wall,
Stories rise and sometimes fall.
With every chuckle in the dark,
The past ignites a tiny spark.

The silliness of growing old,
Reveals the treasures we once told.
Like treasures lost in old disguises,
Each shadow carries sweet surprises.

So let us grin and pull the thread,
And stitch the colors without dread.
For shadows may be all we own,
Yet laughter's light is brightly shown.

An Ode to Impermanence

A single leaf hangs on tight,
In the wind it shakes with fright.
The branches groan with ancient tales,
As laughter drifts where humor pales.

It whispers secrets to the breeze,
A stubborn friend among the trees.
With each gust, a giggle, a sigh,
Wondering when it's time to fly.

Oh, the antics of the seasons,
Wrestling with their fleeting reasons.
In autumn's grip, a show of flair,
One leaf winks, "I'm still up there!"

And when it drops, it won't be sad,
It'll twirl down, oh so mad!
It chuckles at the waiting ground,
"I'll be back — just wait around!"

The Solace of Stubbornness

To stand alone, a daring feat,
This stubborn leaf feels quite elite.
While all its friends have taken flight,
It laughs and plays in fading light.

Oh leaf, you silly, leafy thing,
What joy and nonsense do you bring!
With every gust, you flip and twirl,
A merry dance that makes us whirl.

The branch beneath begins to creak,
Yet you persist with no critique.
"What's an age?" you cackle loud,
To go with grace? Nah, not allowed!

Once winter comes, will you still gloat?
Will you stick on, the last one afloat?
For in your heart, a song's refrain,
This stubbornness is not in vain!

One Last Stand in Decay

Oh what a sight, this fading leaf,
A comedy wrapped in disbelief.
It clings to life with all its might,
Defying seasons, taking flight.

The autumn winds begin to howl,
Yet still it smirks, a cheeky growl.
"Not ready yet," it seems to say,
"As long as I'm here, let's play!"

Around it swirls a world of gold,
Yet here it holds, so brave, so bold.
The others laugh, they can't resist,
This plucky leaf who won't desist.

When winter comes with icy breath,
Will you bemoan your leafy death?
Nay, you'll giggle, giggle away,
For decay's just a new kind of play!

Nature's Heartbeat in Silence

In the hush of twilight's glow,
A leaf hangs on, a hero's show.
Its peers have danced into decay,
But still it sways, come what may.

Tick-tock, the world goes round,
With every breeze, a whispered sound.
"Oh dear life, you're quite a clown,
But I won't let you bring me down!"

The humor of a fading green,
In every wrinkle lies a dream.
It chuckles softly, what a gift,
To find such joy in nature's shift.

So when it falls, it won't be shy,
But flutters down with a gleeful sigh.
"I lived my life, oh what a show!
On this silent stage, I stole the flow!"

Flicker Before the Dark

In the corner of the room, it shakes,
Daring fate with every little quake.
Once vibrant green, now turned to gold,
It whispers secrets only it can hold.

A dust mote waltzes in the light,
While the leaf plots its last flight.
A gentle breeze and it will fall,
Who knew a leaf could have a ball?

Around it gathers dust and fluff,
The shelf seems tired; it's had enough.
A sip of tea, a chuckle, a sneeze,
That leaf just grins, oh, how it teases!

But when the sun begins to fade,
It wonders if that dance was made.
With a shimmy and a laugh that's shy,
The final curtain calls goodbye.

The Change that Haunts the Branch

On a branch so sturdy, so proud and spry,
Sits a leaf that's seen too many a sigh.
Its edges crisp, its color a laugh,
It teeters on humor's flimsy path.

The tree whispers tales of seasons past,
While this lone leaf feels outclassed.
"Am I to be the joker in fall?"
It cackles softly, daring the squall.

A squirrel scurries, glancing up high,
"Hey you, leaf, don't you dare fly!"
But the leaf just giggles, what a tease,
"Catch me if you can, with such a breeze!"

With a bounce, it flutters, what a display,
While the tree shakes its branches, "Not today!"
In the dance of the winds, the leaf takes its chance,
Will it land on the cat? Now, that's a romance!

Time's Soft Footfall on Dead Leaves

As clocks tick gently, the hours wane,
A leaf on the floor feels a bit of strain.
It's seen its pals all tumble down,
But here it stays, a leaf in a gown.

What's this? A shoe? Tap-tap, like fate?
The leaf shivers, oh, it can't wait!
It rolls and it tumbles, what a scene,
Dancing along like a drama queen.

Time murmurs sweetly, "It's fine, my dear,"
While dust collect like an audience here.
A tumble from grace, what a plight,
Yet a giggle escapes, a giddy delight.

At last it settles, and all's anew,
It dreams of the skies, of vibrant hues.
Though time marches, with each little creak,
What a leap to life, for a leaf so meek!

The Fading Touch of Summer's Hand

Once a backdrop of sun, shiny and bright,
Now fading like jokes lost to the night.
That leaf sits, reflecting, oh what a ride,
With memories of summer, it brims with pride.

A gentle breeze and a chuckle, it sighs,
"Did I really wear that silly disguise?"
For every season brings a new tone,
Yet it laughs with glee, never alone.

Its friends now scattered, fallen by chance,
Yet it stands firm, in this awkward dance.
"Who knew I'd be the last to go?"
It winks at time, putting on a show.

As twilight shadows begin to creep,
The leaf does a jig; it won't lose sleep.
With a flick and a twirl, it takes a stand,
In the fading glow of summer's hand.

A Solitary Green

In a world of dust and gray,
There sits a lone, bold bouquet.
Its leaves are few, but oh, so proud,
Waving gently, drawing a crowd.

With whispers soft, it tells a tale,
Of sunny days and stormy gales.
A stubborn sprout, a jester's friend,
Mocking winter as it pretends.

Each wiggle sends a laugh around,
While squirrels ponder, quite confound.
To pluck or not, they stomp and stare,
But miss the punchline in the air.

So here it stands, with cheeky grace,
In a world that's lost its pace.
A solitary green delight,
Bringing humor day and night.

Remnants of Yesterday's Harvest

When autumn played its final card,
The pantry showed a brave facade.
A pickle jar, with lids askew,
And apples too, though quite askew.

A muffin, hard as ancient stone,
While fruit flies dance and moan and groan.
A crumbly muffin's got a quest,
To find a friend who's still the best.

With every nibble, laughter grows,
For who knew magic lived in those?
A feast for mice, a chuckle shared,
Remnants of fun, life unprepared.

So raise a toast to foods gone by,
With flavors bold that make you cry.
While yesterday's harvest fades away,
The humor stays, come what may.

The Quiet Resilience

Amidst the chaos, something waits,
An empty pot, with hopes like fates.
It wears a smile, though all seems lost,
In silence whispers, what a cost!

A rubber plant that's hanging on,
Pretending all is right, not wrong.
With dusty leaves and branches bare,
It's plotting schemes beyond compare.

Oh look! A sprout is peeking through,
A tiny joke that's known by few.
A sign of life, a wink so sly,
That's what they call a laughing high!

So even when the light is dim,
This quiet soul won't let dreams swim.
With every chuckle, roots embrace,
A joyful heart finds its own space.

Shadows of Dimming Light

As evening falls and shadows creep,
The sill's alive, no time for sleep.
A single sprout with bold intent,
In fading light, it won't relent.

With giggles echoing through the night,
It basks in tales of pure delight.
A corner plant with tricks to share,
It chuckles softly, who knows where?

Outside, the chill begins to bite,
But inside, jokes take joyous flight.
The moon's a fan of this small jest,
A comedy that knows no rest.

So let us raise a glass to cheer,
To all the plants that persevere.
In shadows deep, they bloom and glow,
With laughter sprouting, row by row.

Horizons of the Almost Forgotten

In a dusty corner, a book lays fair,
Its spine all crinkled, no reader in there.
The last page whispering, 'Hey, don't you dare!'
While dust bunnies dance without any care.

A mouse in a hat, what a sight to behold,
Reading fine scripts, or so I've been told.
But the plot is so thin, it just won't unfold,
He drinks cheese tea from a cup made of gold.

I wonder what stories might still reside,
In the quiet pages where memories hide.
Each word feels like summer - or is it just pride?
A laugh at the ending, the door open wide.

So here in the silence, let's raise a toast,
To pages and ink that we probably boast.
For in every chuckle, we'll make quite a ghost,
Of tales never told, let's play memory host.

The Fragility of a Faint Memory

A note under the mat, half read and all bent,
Scribbles of laughter and maybe some rent.
I chuckle at how such small things can scent,
The hollows of thought – like time that's well spent.

What was that dream? Ah, slippery and sly,
It danced like a cat, then waved goodbye.
But who needs it now when a pie's fresh and dry?
With crusts full of giggles, we nibble and sigh.

Each memory's flake, could spark a grand cheer,
But so often they float, like feathers unclear.
We summon their shape with each laughter-filled beer,
Then toast to our minds, to what we hold dear!

So here's to the fragments we cherish in jest,
They flutter like leaves, not one is the best.
With humor our armor, we'll laugh, not rest,
And turn the forgotten into a fun fest.

Turned Pages of a Withered Book

In a library's corner, oh what a sight,
A book with whispers, so torn and polite.
The words jump around, like a squirrel's delight,
Searching for snacks in the soft morning light.

One page has hiccups, with laughter it sings,
While others complain of quite serious things.
But mostly they're quiet, like piano strings,
Playing tunes of the past, where the joy often clings.

I read 'bout a hero, who only had shoes,
He stumbled and tumbled, yet never did lose.
For every adventure, he'd find recipes too,
In pages so yellow they could stick to glue!

So let's strum the stories through giggles and grins,
As we frolic on pages where humor begins.
With journeys so wild, no one truly wins,
But those who are laughing, get the greatest spins.

A Canvas Touched by Winter's Breath

On a frosty morning, a canvas resides,
Painted with snowflakes and whimsical rides.
It shivers with laughter, as each one confides,
That winter's cold touch often takes us for strides.

The brush drips like giggles, in splashes of white,
As each drop of color takes wondrous flight.
"Who needs a warm coat?" it chirps with delight,
When frolicking snowmen come out for the night.

A penguin in mittens, with style and with flair,
Sips cocoa while dancing, oblivious to care.
While snow plenitude makes the poor robin stare,
We chuckle at chaos, with nary a scare.

So let's paint together, our canvas anew,
With laughter and cheer, we'll color the view.
For winter's just fun, and it sprinkles like dew,
In a world painted bright, where joy is our cue.

Memories Clinging to Silence

On a lonely branch, a whisper hangs,
The wind jokes softly, as the old tree swangs.
Leaves gossip softly of days gone by,
With every rustle, they stifle a sigh.

An acorn chuckles, it's stuck in a dream,
He wonders if he'll grow, or if it's just a meme.
The squirrels roll their eyes at the old wise trunk,
While dodging all raindrops that smell like funk.

Birds take the stage, a curious show,
Dancing around, putting on a glow.
But the old leaf chuckles, stays stuck in its nook,
Unbothered by seasons, just reading a book.

In this silent humor, the world finds its peace,
Amidst the laughter, the worries cease.
Each moment a treasure, each giggle a gem,
Nature's comedy is a perfect diadem.

When the Last Colors Fade

Autumn's colors, bright like a clown,
Wink and wave from the trees in town.
But as they chuckle, they start to drop,
Thinking, 'Maybe it's time for a swap!'

The red leaves dance with a fiddle's tune,
While the golden ones hum the afternoon.
With every swirl, they bid adieu,
Leaving one leaf stuck, feeling quite blue.

"Oh dear," it thinks, "Am I stuck for good?
With no more colors, how misunderstood!"
It shimmies and shakes, causing some stir,
While the twig next door laughs—what a blur!

In the silence of dusk, it stands all alone,
But it holds its ground like a jester's throne.
Though others have vanished, this one stays bold,
In the fading light, its story unfolds.

A Solstice in Stillness

In the heart of winter, where silence prevails,
One little leaf clings and tells funny tales.
It hitches a ride on the frost's icy breath,
Wondering if it's a dance or a test.

With shadows on snow, it plays hide and seek,
While the sun giggles, peeking like a cheek.
"Where's everyone gone?" it asks with a grin,
"Oh, just off to party, where the warmth doth begin!"

A curious snail makes a slow little crawl,
As the leaf laughs loudly, "Come join the ball!"
With the wind chiming in, a jovial shout,
"Who needs the sun? Let's turn this thing out!"

In stillness, they revel, a quirky tableau,
Celebrating moments of fun in the snow.
With joy in their hearts and laughter in air,
A solstice of silliness, a whimsical affair.

The Final Ember of Autumn's Flame

In a garden of giggles, one ember remains,
While others have flickered, escaping like trains.
It winks at the breeze, a cheeky old spark,
"Doesn't it feel cozy, just waiting till dark?"

The pumpkin parade rolls by with a grin,
Sporting funny masks, letting nonsense begin.
But the ember just chuckles, not afraid to stay,
"It's a comical party; hop on, don't stray!"

As the chill creeps in, it warms up the plot,
Joking with shadows, giving warmth a shot.
"I'm the last of the crew," it gleefully brags,
While the moon rolls its eyes, but secretly lags.

So in this grand finale, let laughter ignite,
With the ember so snug, the world's feeling bright.
In the dance of the dusk, let the funny prevail,
As the last autumn's humor tells a delightful tale.

Final Breath of the Bough

One leaf hung on, it had no plan,
While winds conspired with a sneaky fan.
It swayed and danced in a clumsy clench,
A leaf on a quest, like a strange old wrench.

It watched its friends float down like dreams,
While it clung tight, defying the schemes.
'I'm not done yet!' it seemed to declare,
With bravado unmatched—like it just didn't care.

Each gust of wind was a ticklish tease,
This leaf was bold, as bold as you please.
"Why fall," it mused, "when I can just swing?
I'm a thrill-seeking leaf! What fun I can bring!"

But time ticked on, as it surely must,
Even stubborn leaves will turn to dust.
So it twirled one last time in the breeze,
And waved goodbye with an awkward sneeze!

Dancer in the Vitamin Light

In morning's glow, it took the stage,
A single leaf, a leafy sage.
With sunlight streaming like golden beams,
It jived and twirled in its vibrant dreams.

It leaped and laughed in a wobbly way,
Practicing for a leafy ballet.
"Watch me now!" it shouted with glee,
As bugs and birds all came to see.

With stretches wide and pirouettes grand,
The vitamin beams gave a helping hand.
"I can show you moves you've never seen!
I'm the star of the branch! I'm the dancing queen!"

But soon it tired, its moves went slow,
The spotlight dimmed, it high-fived a crow.
With a flourish and bow, it took a rest,
A dancer retired, though it did its best!

A Solitary Gesture of Farewell

One leaf stood proud, a lone little star,
As autumn waved, it declared, "No far!"
Its friends had flitted, with laughter and cheer,
While it clung tight, refusing to veer.

"I'm waiting for a bus," it said with a grin,
A leaf on a journey—let the fun begin!
It stretched and yawned, with leafly flair,
An unlikely hero in the cool, crisp air.

But buses came and left, what a fuss!
No ticket in hand, it pondered, "What's the rush?"
A gesture so bold in its leafy retreat,
Just waving goodbye to its own silly beat.

Then came a gust, oh what a fright!
"Is that my ride?" it squeaked in delight.
But off it flew, with a giggle, a whirl,
A solitary leaf—a farewell twirl!

The Awkward Embrace of Winter

The frost crept in, with a chilly grin,
While one leaf trembled, feeling quite thin.
"I really thought," it muttered with dread,
"That winter would be a nice place to tread."

It clung to its branch with a grip like glue,
As snowflakes giggled and fell right on cue.
"I'm not finished yet, I have tales to tell!"
But winter just snickered, "You know it too well."

With every gust, it wobbled and wove,
An awkward embrace, this leaf had to prove.
"I'm the warmest leaf in this frosty parade,
Come join the fun, let's begin the charade!"

But alas, it slipped in a frosty embrace,
With snowflakes around it—a silly case.
The winter chuckled, "Wasn't that good?
Next time maybe, try not hanging on to wood!"

The Final Whisper of the Breeze

A single green hangs on tight,
Defying all with silly might.
The wind just laughs, a cheeky tease,
"Hey buddy, let go, it's time to freeze!"

The others fell, a jolly dance,
But one stays firm—oh, what a chance!
"Stay with me," the branch does plead,
While squirrels watch, their eyes do greed.

The world spins on, indifferent, sure,
While leaves below decay and cure.
That stubborn leaf just wiggles on,
Like it's the star of an old-time song!

And when it drops, oh what a sight,
A leaf that thought it won the night.
With laughter shared by all around,
That final whisper, lost, yet found.

A Remnant's Quiet Grace

Oh leaf, you cling with all your might,
Each gust of wind a playful fright.
The branches shake, the world is jest,
"Just drop already, take your rest!"

In autumn's chill, you're quite the tease,
Refusing nature's gentle squeeze.
The sun peeks out, a doting friend,
"Hurry up, dear! This must end!"

You're not alone, there's dirt below,
Laughing softly, your time will go.
As winter comes with frosty frown,
You sway and dance, the last in town.

But when you fall, it's not goodbye,
You'll rest in peace, just watch the sky.
A story told, a wink, a grace,
A memory left, just in the space.

The Hushed Farewell of the Season

One leafy friend, so bold and loud,
Outshining all beneath the crowd.
The trees conspire, their plots are sly,
"Let's give this star a reason why!"

With wrinkled edges, it won't budge,
While whispers say, "Just take a judge."
The world below is a leafless spree,
Yet you remain, oh sight to see!

The frost arrives, but you just grin,
Expecting fruitcake and a tin.
"Holidays are here, why bother me?
I'm the last act of this old tree!"

And when you finally hit the ground,
The echo fades, a chuckle sound.
For in your plunge, we see the jest,
An ending that won't soon rest.

Time's Reluctant Hand

Time ticks on, leaves drift away,
With every gust, they seem to play.
One stands strong, a comedian's dream,
A punchline waiting, it might seem.

The breeze rolls in, a cheeky cheer,
"Come on, leaf, let's make this clear!"
The branches laugh, a raucous clan,
While you hang tight—oh, be a fan!

With every storm, you play aloof,
"Who needs the ground? I'm the goof!"
And while your mates turn brown and pale,
You're there, a quirky fairy tale.

At last, you drop, a final dance,
A moment brief, a leaf's last chance.
You've played your part, now take a bow,
And let the world have fun somehow!

Remnants of Light in the Dark

In a room full of shadows, men gather,
One brave soul yells, "Don't check, it's a lather!"
While the dust bunnies chuckle, hiding in pride,
The lone bulb flickers, it's their only guide.

With cups raised high, they toast to the gloom,
Yet the fridge hums softly, breaking the doom.
A snack is their savior, a light in the dead,
Even rotten old cheese gives hope to the spread.

The brave ones still venture, but only one stays,
Retreating to corners where daylight decays.
In the end, it twinkles, their laughter a spark,
Like a firefly's dance in the depths of the dark.

So here's to the moments we wrestle with fate,
Where even the jokes grown stale, find a mate.
With humor and hope, we chip away fright,
In the remnants of light, we laugh through the night.

The Quiet Call of Oblivion

A chair creaks beneath an age-old soul,
Whispering tales of a grand pot of coal.
In the far corner sits a sock, lone and gray,
Imagining careers it never will play.

As dust gathers thick like an actor's broad gown,
The cat swipes a napkin, feeling like a clown.
With each little rumble, the old folks tickle,
The air filled with laughter, and the room feels fickle.

Then silence erupts, as chips fall in quick,
A tumble of popcorn, a slapstick trick.
Peeking through curtains, the sun fakes a grin,
Wrapped in the chaos, the fun will begin.

In this quiet abyss where the memory winks,
The unlucky sock dreams, and the old chair thinks.
It's a show of absurdity, play-by-play,
Where oblivion's whispers boggle the fray.

An Epilogue to Nature's Ballad

Once in the woods, the squirrels did prance,
Hiding their treasures, oh what a chance!
All thoughts of the acorns were not what they seemed,
It's hard to stay humble when nature's redeemed.

A brittle branch snaps, and a giggle escapes,
Echoes of critters in outrageous capes.
While leaves toss and turn in a dizzying swirl,
The critters conspire, and nature's a whirl.

The owl in the tree rolls its big, wise eyes,
"Oh please, with this madness, I'm ready for pies!"
But atop the high branches, they all swing and sway,
In the fervor of nature's unpredictable play.

Though the seasons shall change, no dismal end found,
The humor in chaos keeps laughter renowned.
As an epilogue echoes among every thrall,
Nature's grand stories, amusing for all.

The Softness of Goodbye

In the corner sits an old and soft chair,
Whispering secrets of those who sat there.
With cushions all frayed, and threads that fray more,
It won't let them leave—oh, it's such a bore!

A blanket, once cozy, now drapes like a ghost,
Hugging the pillows like it's missing its host.
Gossiping softly with dust in its seams,
The myths of the residents' long-gone dreams.

A fragile farewell, as the clock ticks away,
Each second a giggle, then back to dismay.
While mice plan their feast on the crumbs of the past,
Goodbyes here are soft, a sweet spell cast.

So here's to the echoes that flutter and sigh,
To the laughter and whimsy we can't let fly.
Though farewells may linger, they don't steal the show,
In the softness of goodbye, we cherish the glow.

Threads of Promise in Dying Shades

In a cozy nook, where time stands still,
A single green musters up the will.
It sways and giggles, oh what a sight,
Wishing for friends to join in the slight.

Hiding from dust, refusing to fade,
Its color's a prank, a bold charade.
With charm so bright, it plays at the art,
Of piquing the laughter in every heart.

Tales of resilience wrapped in its veins,
A story of joy that lightly remains.
With each chirp and chuckle, it shows with glee,
How funny it is to cling to a tree.

So here's to the green, so quirky and spry,
That makes all the others just wither and die.
A hero of humor on shelves piled high,
In a world full of dreams, we'll never say bye.

The Solitary Sway of Time

One leaf alone, a jester near death,
Winks with a smile, as it saves its breath.
It dances and spins, a world on its tip,
Making the woodwork chuckle and rip.

While others just crumbled and faded away,
This one puts on quite the entertaining display.
A delicate hero, a stubborn old chap,
Caught in the wind with a comical flap.

It shouts to the world, 'Hey, look at me!'
With its wobble and jig, it's laughing with glee.
A stand-up performer on nature's vast stage,
It flips through the air, defying old age.

So here's to the leaf that refuses to pout,
In a season of change, it's fun all about.
With humor and charm, it's our trusty muse,
Turning the mundane to joyful news.

A Canvas of Rhythmic Decay

On a table birthing tales so absurd,
Sits a lone leaf with wisdom deferred.
It jives with the dust bunnies, sharp and spry,
Reminds us to laugh, even as time flies by.

Pencils montaged, sketches undone,
It spins bravely, joining the fun.
Each crinkle and curl is a dance in disguise,
A comedy sketch written through sighs.

With a flick and a flit, it stirs the air,
Bringing bouts of giggles with colorful flair.
In the pit of the room, it's the life of the bash,
While all older leaves lie and quietly crash.

So let's raise a toast to this vivid delight,
For laughter's the color in shades of twilight.
With every faux pas, it proves with a grin,
That joy is a leaf that we keep tucked in.

Echoes of the Green Past

Among dusty tomes, a green tale unfolds,
With laughter echoing through ancient old molds.
Just one remaining, it hangs by a thread,
A symbol of life where all others have fled.

It pokes fun at the seasons that swiftly have passed,
Whispers to shadows of summers amassed.
"Oh come now," it chuckles, "don't take it to heart,
With humor, we flourish, life's not too apart."

A wily old leaf, over the edge of a page,
Winking at readers, delighting the sage.
It flutters and flounces, a joker's bright hue,
Reminding us always to laugh at what's true.

So let's tip our hats to this sprightly old grieve,
For joy and resilience trickle within eve.
In a world full of changes, it flutters and beams,
Reminding us all to hold fast to our dreams.

Hope Against the Frost

In the chill of morning's grasp,
A greenish hue stands tall and proud,
The frost rolls in, a silent gasp,
Yet one odd sprout denies the crowd.

Around it flurries all the doubt,
But here it clings with silly glee,
While nature shakes her head about,
"You really think you're meant to be?"

Each snowflake whispers, "Time to drop!"
Yet there it wobbles, like a clown,
And every poke just makes it bop,
A stubborn joke in winter's gown.

So here's to all who stand the pain,
A little odd, yet full of cheer,
For laughter in a world of rain,
Is just as bright, it seems, my dear.

The Canvas of Letting Go

A canvas bright, a vibrant hue,
With swirls and curls of autumn's art,
Yet one strange leaf, in bold debut,
Holds tight—oh, bless its little heart!

The brush of fate just takes a sweep,
It shakes and rattles with the breeze,
But this one leaf, it will not leap,
It sticks like gum beneath the fees!

As nature yells, "Just fall away!"
This leaf insists, "I'll stay awhile!"
A comic scene in bright dismay,
As winter waits with frosty smile.

So grab your paint and stroke with flair,
For every leaf has tales to spill,
A funny life to rip or tear,
To dance on air or sit quite still.

Surrendering to the Stillness

In quietude, the world prepares,
The branches bare, the shadows stretched,
Yet flagging free, an odd affair,
One leaf hangs on, a plan unmatched!

The wind just snickers, clouds conspire,
To give this sprout a gentle nudge,
With every breath, to lose the fire,
But down it clings, as if to judge!

The silence tugs, the cold recedes,
It's stubbornness—a funny thing,
While all around in muted weeds,
This rebel leaf won't hear the ring.

The ground awaits with open arms,
As winter scowls and comes to call,
Yet with a twirl, it waves with charms,
And laughs away the frosty fall.

When Seasons Whisper Goodbye

When seasons blink with cheeky eyes,
And time decides to shift the stage,
One leaf defies the whispered sighs,
It shimmies on, an aging sage!

The winds declare, "It's time to leave!"
But this leaf dances, full of zest,
Proclaiming boldly, "I believe!"
A bit absurd, but feels the best!

Winter grumbles, "Don't you know?"
With icy breath, it tries to sway,
Yet laughter rings, a playful show,
As one leaf winks and laughs, "Not today!"

So grab your coats, the skies are gray,
And let that leaf remind us all,
In every shift, come what may,
A hint of joy will still enthrall.

Fading Pages of Time

Once a sprightly volume, bold and bright,
Now it's slightly dog-eared, faded from light.
Dust bunnies dance where the laughter was loud,
Sipping old coffee, but still feeling proud.

The chapters are shallow, the plots all a mess,
It feels like a sitcom, but with one less guess.
The bookmarks, they giggle, lost in the fray,
As the dust jackets whisper, 'Where's the next play?'

Old ink is a comedy, a slight fading jive,
Every turn of the page, it struggles to thrive.
Yet in this decay, a charm all its own,
A bookworm's delight, in pages it's grown.

So here's to the stories, both quirky and strange,
With their colorful characters, all just a bit deranged.
On this dusty old shelf, let laughter abound,
In the fading of pages, new joy can be found.

Whisper of Autumn's End

A raucous old tome with a spine of pure cheer,
Writes tales of grand adventures and never a tear.
Yet whispers of autumn float in with a crunch,
Leaves and old covers play games during lunch.

The plot's a little lost, like socks in a wash,
Heroes trip over pumpkins, and villains just squash.
Every line has a giggle, each pause a keen poke,
As the pages reveal secrets with every bloke joke.

Dust settles in piles like a gathering crew,
Plot twists on the counter, it's déjà vu!
Yet here on the shelf, it hums a sweet tune,
With laughter and joy, in this old autumn's swoon.

So raise up a glass to the tales that we spin,
With giggles and snickers, let the fun begin!
As the last leaf tumbles it's still full of cheer,
In this autumnal tale, we won't disappear.

New Beginnings in Decay

Once a grand epic, now a comic strip,
Hilarious hiccups, each sentence a quip.
The storyline's wobbly, but who needs a guide?
In the circus of words, let's just take a ride!

The turning of pages akin to a dance,
Dust mites can shimmy while words take a chance.
Old covers unravel with laughter and glee,
As the book's got its quirks, let it sunny bee!

The chapters turn goofy, like socks with no pairs,
Sir Plot Tweak a lot wonders; do we need repairs?
In this library circus of tales so quirky,
Every last giggle makes our hearts feel sparky.

So let's make a toast to the jesters of prose,
With puns and with jests, let creativity flow.
In the dancing of paper, find beauty in flaws,
And remember, dear reader, to laugh without pause.

Echoes of a Withering Season

A novel once sprightly, now tattered and curled,
Tells tales of a time when it ruled the world.
Each page a comedy, written with glee,
In this saga of wisdom, come share a cup of tea.

The cover's a relic, the spine's got a twist,
And characters ponder, 'Is there more on the list?'
With each funny scene, we chuckle in turn,
As autumn leaves whirl and the pages we yearn.

The laughter is bellowing, the punchline is near,
In the echoes of stories that we all hold dear.
A book on the shelf with a wink and a nudge,
Inviting us closer, saying, "Hey, no grudge!"

So here's to the tales that wane and re-bloom,
In the fade of the season, we let laughter loom.
Embrace every giggle, let joy take the stage,
In the echoes of laughter, we'll never age.

Ephemeral Beauty in Shadows

In the corner it clings, with a twist of fate,
Its friends have dropped off, isn't it great?
A leaf with a story, of days long past,
Hanging on high, it's not going fast.

The wind gives a giggle, a playful breeze,
It dances around, aiming for ease.
"Look at me! I'm holding on tight!"
The other leaves watch, oh what a sight!

A spider spins webs, a glimmering trap,
While squirrels conspire, in their secret map.
They chuckle and chatter, all while it sways,
"What a dumb leaf, to waste all its days!"

And yet, in the gloom where the shadows drape,
This silly old leaf is the best kind of shape.
It flutters and flails, with a spirit so bold,
An odd little wonder, worth more than gold.

The Lonely Note of Change

A single note lingers on a branch stark,
Beneath the fading sun, it leaves quite a mark.
Its buddies have fluttered, not one's inside,
Just a lonely tune with nowhere to glide.

The cats sneak around, with a curious gaze,
It teeters and totters, in a dizzying maze.
"Why don't you join us?" they purr with delight,
The leaf just chuckles, "I've got all night!"

A butterfly flits, looking sharp and spry,
"Come dance with me now! Don't be shy!"
But the leaf just chuckles, "I'll pass, I'll stay,
I'm the last little buddy, what can I say?"

Each gust of wind brings a fresh little laugh,
As it sways and jives for its own photograph.
In the gallery of change, it's the final frame,
A quirky little gem, too proud to be tame.

Season of the Almost Forgotten

Once a lush kingdom, now a tale thin,
A hero still hangs, though the fight wears thin.
The world spins and twirls, much to its glee,
But our brave little soldier won't tumble with ease.

Time drips like honey, soft, slow, and sweet,
While critters below share their autumnal treats.
"Come down from there!" they squeak in their singsong,
But the leaf just grins, "I'm defying the wrong!"

It watches the world as it spins in its dance,
Not quite a leaf, and not quite a chance.
"I'll hold down the fort, till winter's parade,
Then I'll slip with a laugh into snow's silky shade!"

Each clock chimes a tune, slightly off-key,
As the comedy rolls on, so dark and so free.
With a wink and a wiggle, it stays overhead,
The last act of autumn, quite poorly but said.

The Long Goodbye to Green

A farewell so grand, yet a comic affair,
As colors descend, from bright green to bare.
With shades of confusion, it wobbles in place,
Trying to linger, it's lost in a race.

The trees whisper secrets with chuckles and sighs,
"I'm still in my prime!" the leaf softly cries.
But even the chirps of the chirping old birds,
Soothe it with laughter, in comical words.

"Let's paint you all gold!" the sunset insists,
Yet, it dodges the brushes, with a flick of its wrist.
"Not ready for change, I'm quite fine right here,
With my sweater of green, I have naught to fear!"

Yet seasons are crafty, a whimsical thief,
It's time for the show, the grand leaf motif.
With a fluttering giggle, it dances to ground,
A long goodbye chuckle, in colors profound.

Imprints of Life on Silent Pages

In a dusty nook, the stories wait,
Whispering tales of a peculiar fate.
A book once read, now home to dust,
Its pages curled, a silent mistrust.

On a shelf high up, a far-off place,
Lives a character with a quirky face.
Stuck in a plot no one can find,
Hoping for readers, his heart intertwined.

Old bookmarks flutter like lost little birds,
While plotlines meander without any words.
An author's dream, a plot in a trance,
Hoping one day, someone will glance.

So here's to the shelf, and its imprints dear,
Where laughter echoes, and stories appear.
Each spine a laugh, each page a song,
In the grand library where all quirks belong.

The Linger of Shadows and Light

Beneath the beams where dust motes play,
Shadows linger like they've lost their way.
A heart-shaped lamp with a bulb that flickers,
Casting strange shapes, and oh, the snickers!

Two squirrels debate on a window ledge,
One steals a nut, the other a pledge.
The sunlight chuckles, "What a fine scene!"
While the curtain sighs, looking quite keen.

Ghosts of the past throw a shadowy dance,
Creating odd moments, a funny romance.
In the play of light, all quirks come alive,
As even the dust bunnies seem to thrive.

So let us rejoice in the shadows bright,
For laughter is found in the edge of night.
Where life gives us wit, and stories take flight,
In the linger of shadows, there's always delight.

One Last Whisper of Gold

Once there was treasure, a shimmer, a glow,
In the forgotten chest, down in the low.
A coin sat grinning, with a cheeky flair,
"Who'd have thought I'd end up here with hair?"

It told of journeys, through lands far and wide,
With pirates and mermaids, and adventures that slide.
But here on the shelf, it feels out of place,
Dreaming of life at a peddler's pace.

"What's that?" it hears—a whispering sound,
Is it fate or fortune, or just spinning round?
Like a stand-up comic, it waits for a chuckle,
"C'mon, pick me up, let's shake off this buckle!"

So here it will sit, till a bold hand is brave,
To uncover the laughter in life's gentle wave.
For even a whisper can be worth its gold,
In the tales we spin, and the fun we behold.

Wistful Revelations in Rust

Old tools hang quietly, with handles worn,
Each notch and crevice with memories adorned.
A hammer grumbles, "What happened to me?"
"Once I was strong, now I'm rusty and free!"

The saw's in a corner, with a crooked grin,
"Did you hear the rumors? A new age begins!"
While the wrench just chuckles, "I've seen it all,
From flashy new gadgets to the great tool hall."

A toolbox from yonder, its lock is askew,
Trapped in nostalgia of when tools were few.
"We were heroes once, now it's all a fuss,
In wistful revelations, we quietly rust."

So let's raise a toast to the tools of the past,
In laughter and tales, their legacy cast.
For every old tool has a story to share,
In the clinks and the clatters, let humor declare.

The Last Glimmer of Days Past

A distant chuckle, time slips away,
Old memories dance, they laugh and sway.
In dusty corners, a treasure remains,
With stories to tell, despite all the pains.

When shadows stretch long, and light starts to fade,
An old joke resurfaces, laughter cascades.
Underneath cobwebs, a grin starts to sprout,
As if to remind us, there's fun hanging out!

The past is a puzzle, each piece out of place,
Yet we wear it proudly, a comical grace.
Where giggles and gaffes twirl in delight,
And memories shine, like stars in the night.

So here's to the moments, both silly and quaint,
The foolish times that we think we can't paint.
In every last glimmer, a flash we can feel,
With laughter still echoing, time's perfect seal.

Fragments Hanging in Suspense

Hanging like laundry, thoughts twist and twirl,
In the wind of the moment, like flags flags unfurl.
Oh, the tales they could tell if only they spoke,
Of giggles and mishaps, a whimsical cloak.

With fabric of laughter, they flutter with glee,
While time mumbles softly, "Oh dear, wait for me!"
A tapestry woven of joy and of jest,
In the cloth of our lives, we stitch up the best.

Each thread represents a misadventure we've known,
Keeping secrets close, though their truth may be shown.
A medley of moments, absurd and diverse,
Unraveled in fun, like a well-versed verse.

So here's to those fragments, so silly and bright,
Hanging in suspense, like a joke at first light.
Letting time tick on as we smile and we grin,
Celebrating the chaos, where laughter begins.

Tenderness in the Twilight Air

In the twilight's embrace, the chuckles grow bold,
With mischief and joy, our stories unfold.
Wistful whispers float on the breeze,
As memories tangle like mischievous leaves.

Through twilight's soft glow, a chuckle appears,
Tickling the senses, it banishes fears.
Every sigh of the evening holds laughter inside,
As we cherish the moments, the warmth turns the tide.

Though shadows may creep, and the day's nearly done,
We find joy in laughter, for that's how we've won.
With hugs and with smiles, let's treasure the night,
For tenderness lingers, and everything's right.

So let's raise a glass to the laughter we share,
In the twilight's sweet kiss, we release every care.
With each giggle we utter, we brighten the air,
As long as there's laughter, we'll always be there.

The Dimming Joy of a Branch

A branch in the wind, dancing ever so slight,
With leaves that still giggle, in fading daylight.
Their rustle a chuckle, a whisper of cheer,
As if to say, "Hey, don't shed any tears!"

Though some may be leaving, they're waving goodbye,
With a wink and a grin, in the sunny blue sky.
A funny farewell, with a jig and a spin,
Reminding us softly that soon we'll begin.

The last of the laughter clings tight to the wood,
As branches swap stories, oh, how they've stood!
With shadows for friends, and roots deep in mirth,
They chuckle together, embracing their worth.

So here's to the joy in the dimming of light,
To the dance of the leaves in their quirky delight.
For in every farewell, a promise will rise,
With laughter and love, we'll continue the ties.

www.ingramcontent.com/pod-product-compliance
Lightning Source LLC
Chambersburg PA
CBHW070315120526
44590CB00017B/2685